The Official Foxtail Book

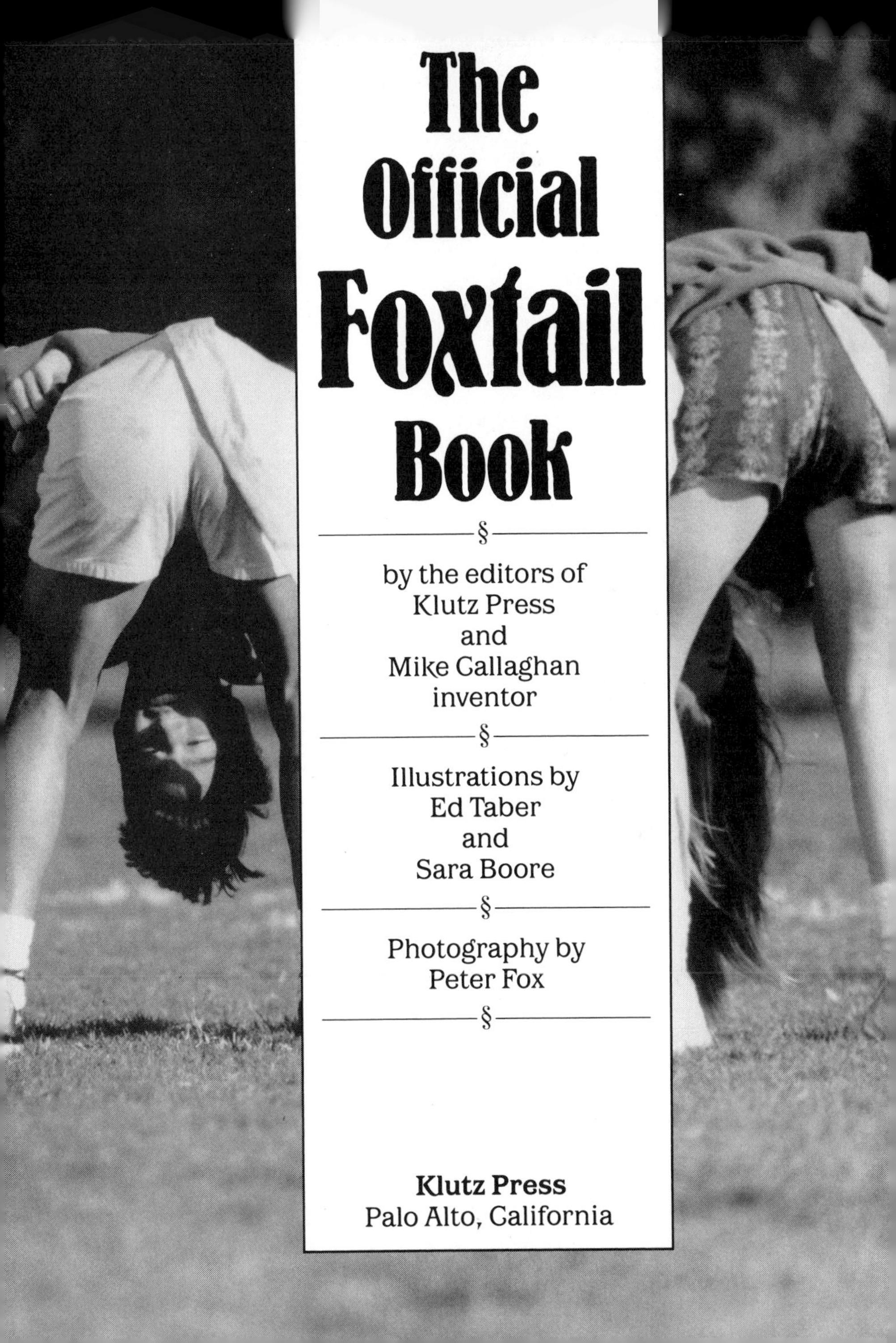

The Official Foxtail Book

§

by the editors of
Klutz Press
and
Mike Callaghan
inventor

§

Illustrations by
Ed Taber
and
Sara Boore

§

Photography by
Peter Fox

§

Klutz Press
Palo Alto, California

Acknowledgements:
Don Fogle and Mag Hughes of
We Care Alternative Sports,
West Linn, Oregon

Illustrations:
Sara Boore (instructive art)
Ed Taber (cartoons)

Production:
Eileen Stolee

The Foxtail flying sporting good is
protected under U.S. patent number
4826179.
"Foxtail" is a trademark of Mike
Callaghan. The trademark "Foxtail"
is used throughout the text of this
book exclusively in reference to the
Foxtail flying sporting good.

Published by Klutz Press
Manufactured in the U.S.A.

Write Us

Klutz Press is an independent
publisher located in Palo Alto,
California and staffed entirely by
real human beings. We would love to
hear your comments regarding this,
or any of our books. Klutz Press, 2121
Staunton Court, Palo Alto, CA, 94306

Additional Copies

For the location of your nearest Klutz
retailer, call (415) 857-0888. If they
should all be regrettably out of stock,
the entire library of Klutz books, as well
as a variety of other things we happen
to like, are available in our mail order
catalogue. See back pages for ordering
information.

4 1 5 8 5 7 0 8

ISBN 1-878257-021

Table of Contents

Active Part

Weight

THE game of catch is such a fundamental game that its roots have intertwined themselves in the human genetic code. Scientists will one day discover which strand of human DNA contains the "throw-and-catch" gene but in the meantime we do know that it is a dominant trait in all human beings. (Not to mention selected other animals. Consider the obsessive stick dog whose DNA helix appears to be made of nothing except "please-throw-me-a-stick" genes).

Evolving right alongside the game of catch is, of course, that all-time sporting good invention, The Ball.

Almost unquestionably the ball came out of early mankind's search for a user-friendly rock. We humbly believe that the Foxtail is nothing less than a long-overdue rung up that same evolutionary ladder. To use the language of geometry for a second (but only a second), the good and bad thing about a ball is that it is a point. A Foxtail, on the other hand, is a line. And since catching is the art of mid-air interception, the advantages of grabbing for a line (rather than a point) are self-evident.

At the other end of the game, the throwing end, the Foxtail again also turns out to be a far more satisfying tool. The extra leverage of the nylon tail basically turbo-charges the ball. This is the "David vs. Goliath Effect." You'll notice it immediately. In fact, when you first go out to play a game of Foxtail, you'll probably spend half your time just spinning it. (It's so satisfying to rev it up). Actually one or two turns is all you need to get your Foxtail up to top speed.

There are dozens of well-tested Foxtail games here in this book, but there are undoubtedly legions more that are waiting to be discovered. Since the Foxtail is such a brand-new ball, the field is wide open for further discovery and invention. We invite you to take the Foxtail's newness and use it as an opportunity to think in new ways and invent new games. And if your neighborhood falls in love with your new game, send it in to us. We'll try it right here in our corporate parking lot and, if it passes our Fun-o-Meter test, we'll put it in the next printing.

KLUTZ PRESS
2121 STAUNTON CT.
PALO ALTO CA. 94306

A Word About Safety:

The Foxtail is made of top-grain cowhide covering a 4-ounce sponge rubber ball. Play with it carefully. Use as much concern for other players, by-standers, and innocent windows as you would with any other flying sporting good.

———————————————— § ————————————————

The voice of experience: Foxtails float, so you won't lose them in a lake, but they also have a gut-level attraction for trees. Their tails will inevitably wrap around high branches and you will be left fuming on the ground. One solution which has worked most of the time for us: Tie a string to another Foxtail and heave it up after the first one. The second

Foxtail will hopefully get tangled nearby and you can use the string to shake the first one down. (Of course, there was the time that the string broke for us and we nearly lost *both* Foxtails).

In the same vein, watch for telephone and electric wires. We once lost a Foxtail for a long day and a half while we waited for the wind to unwrap it off a telephone wire.

The Law of the Foxtail

§

ALL THROWS AND ALL CATCHES MUST BE MADE BY THE TAIL ONLY

§

There are no points awarded for catching or throwing by the ball. Think of the ball as nothing but a weight. The active part of the Foxtail, the only part that you should worry about, is the tail.

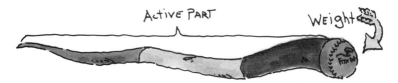

Active Part   Weight

The Basic Foxtail Toss

All throws are made by spinning and releasing the nylon tail. Grabbing and throwing by the ball doesn't even get you a zero. Hold it by the middle color and twirl it three or four times before letting go.

You can spin it at your side or over your head ("lariat style"). Either way, keep your eye on your target, step forward and release in a lob. Line drives can come later.

Your first few attempts will not be terribly accurate. Do not be disappointed. If you like, shift your grip up a little higher, towards the ball, and slow down a bit. In general, you can get better accuracy by holding the Foxtail high (towards the ball). You can get more distance by holding it low (towards the tail). After you become a Foxtail Awesome Person of course, you'll be able to hold it low and still thread a needle at 80 yards, but that state of grace doesn't come for a little while.

The Side Spin and Release
Step by Step

1.   **2.**

One glitch that will affect your accuracy is the way you release the Foxtail. This seems almost too obvious to mention, but it actually plays a big role. If the tail of the Foxtail wraps in your fingers, hanging up for even a millisecond, it'll throw your aim off by embarrassing amounts. Little kids who are afflicted with the "wrong-way syndrome," in which the Foxtail goes backward rather than the intended forward, are just having trouble letting go of it. A lesser degree of the same problem is at the root of many throws just off the mark.

3.   **4.**

Which way to spin it (at your side or over your head) is your choice. The overhead spin should be inclined a bit so that you can throw lobs with it, but it's basically every bit as accurate as the side-spin. The side-spin can give you higher lobs, and it's obviously the only way to throw it straight up, but after just a little bit of practice, you should be able to switch between the two of them just as a tennis player switches between forehand and backhand.

Overhead Spin and Release
Step by Step

1.   **2.**

The Basic Foxtail Catch

First of all, since I can't say this enough, let me say it again: All catches have to be made by the tail only. In the games described here, that rule is defined strictly. Even if you just touch the ball on your way to making a grab on the tail, that's called a ball-foul. No catch.

So how do you make clean grabs? Foxtail is like life: Timing is everything. As the Foxtail goes winging by, aim for a point just behind the ball. You probably won't get it, but if you aim high, you'll have 30 inches margin for error. That should be plenty. In most of the games, points are awarded depending on which color is grabbed. The hardest grabs (getting the highest points) are on the top color, the one right by the ball.

Catch it
hERE —.

NEVER — NEVER—NEVER—
NEVER—NEVER—NEVER Catch it hERE.

For screaming line drives, or monster sky balls, wait for a milli-second and stab for the Foxtail from behind, after it's passed you. You'll avoid a lot of ball fouls that way and make some high grabs that would be very difficult otherwise.

For kids who are a little too young to manage a mid-flight grab, play with the one-bounce rule. Wait for the ball to hit, and then grab it before it bounces again. Most of the games work fine with this simple change.

Nine Variations

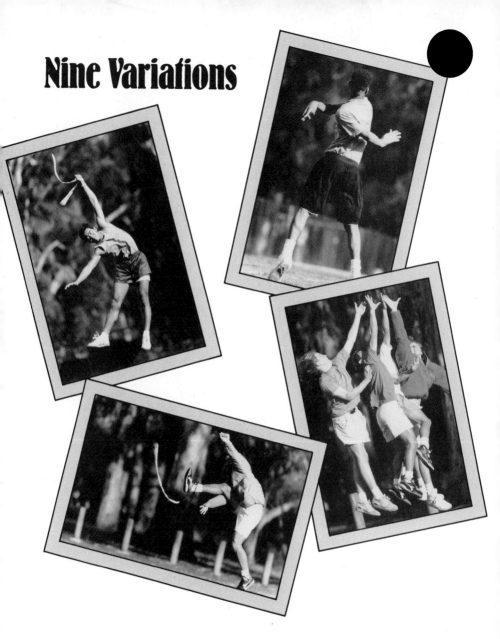

Here are nine ways to add a little bite to the honored
game of catch. Most of them can be played with any
number in almost any size space. Many of them can be
tailored for younger kids by allowing any catch to be
made on a hop (the "One Bounce Rule").

Steps

Any number can play. If you have more than two, everyone should spread out equidistantly. The object of the game is to throw strikes. If someone throws wide to you, and you have to move to make the catch, count your steps. The number you get is the thrower's penalty and it goes on his score sheet. As soon as a player gets to a thousand, they have to step out. Last in is the winner.

Horse Tail

Any number can play. Toss the Foxtail from one player to another (all tosses have to be reasonably accurate lobs, no fastballs, please). The idea is to make ridiculously

difficult catches: behind the back, under the leg, top color, head bounce then grab … etc. etc. After a successful "wonder-catch," the player immediately after you has to do the same. If he or she fails, they get the letter "H" (then "O", then "R", then "S"…). If they succeed, then the player after them has to copy it (unless it's back to your turn, in which case you can do whatever you want).

First to "HORSE" has to step out. Last in receives the free milkshake everyone else promised when the game began.

P.S. You can also permit "wonder-throws" that come from between the legs, behind the back, backwards etc. If the wonder-throw is catchable by the person to whom it was aimed, then that person must duplicate it (catchably!). For the ultimate challenge, make a wonder- catch, and then wonder-throw it to the next player. Now they have to do both to avoid a letter.

Catching by the Colors

Players toss the Foxtail back and forth from any distance they want. The catcher has to catch by the same color that the thrower used (seam catches count as the color above them). And to keep the colors moving around, every throw has to be on a different color than the previous *two* throws.

This is a good one-bounce game for younger kids. Keeping score is optional.

Consecutives

Strictly a two-person game, probably the only one that might be able to get you into the Guinness book some day.

Back off from your partner about 20 giant steps. Scratch a line in the dirt (or put your jacket down if you're on the street). Your partner does the same. The area between the lines (or jackets) is no-man's-land. You can't throw or catch from no-man's-land.

Start tossing and catching. Don't cross the line and don't miss. The record around here is 612 without a miss, blatant ball-foul, or crossing of the line. If you can beat that, drop us a line. We'll put your card on the board.

P.S. A "ball-foul" occurs when your hand hits the ball but you still end up hanging onto the tail. It's a no-no.

One Motion

This is a good variation to pull out if you're tossing the Foxtail around in a large group. It keeps the game really moving and if a misguided throw gets away from somebody, it's no problem. In a big enough circle, somebody'll get it.

The only rule is simple. With the same motion that you make the catch, you have to make  the throw. One smooth swing. No regripping, no switching of hands, no nothing. Catch and throw. One motion.

Slap Catch

Although the Law of the Foxtail states that it is illegal to catch by the ball, in this particular game it is OK to hit it. But just for this game only. Here's how it goes.

You'll need at least 4 players. Break up into even teams. Start tossing the Foxtail back and forth. Since there are no out-of-bounds lines, the throws have to be directed towards someone. If the throw comes directly to you, you're not allowed to catch it. You have to slap or bounce it to someone else on your team who either catches it (by the tail only!) or slaps it on to someone else. We play it either way.

Thou Shalt Throw & Catch
BY
THE TAIL
ONLY
THE LAW OF THE FOXTAIL

Bounce Catch

A great game for venting frustration. Any age can play.
The rules are simple: On an asphalt playground, slam the
Foxtail down so that it takes a high bounce. Then, before
it bounces again, your partner has to catch it, and slam it
back. Very satisfying.

Sky Juggling

This is a group juggling show. Those of us who sell Foxtails love it. You'll need one more Foxtail than you've got players. And you can play with any number from two up. For explanation's sake, we'll say it's just Boris and Natasha playing. Boris is holding two Foxtails, Natasha one. Boris throws one of his straight up, sky-high. Natasha circles underneath it, preparing to make the catch. As it peaks and starts to drop, Natasha throws her Foxtail straight up and catches the incoming. Now Boris is back on the job. He has to throw his and catch hers. In this order.

On it goes. At no time should anyone be caught holding two Foxtails. The more people you have, the more fun it is. Count consecutives; this is not an easy catch. (Hint: It's all in the throw. Very high, very accurate, and timed just right.)

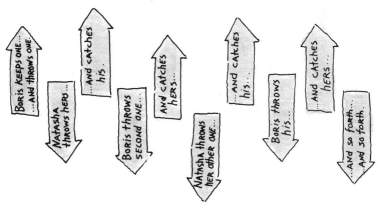

Foxtail ™

The Tournament Rules

21

For most people, it takes quite a little while before even the basic game of Foxtail catch starts to seem routine. But when that day arrives, we want you to be ready. Here are the rules to Foxtail 21, the fundamental game of the sport. No matter what your skill level is, you can play it (or one of its variations) happily for the rest of your Foxtail career.

How to Figure Out Who Goes First

This is easy. Both players approach one another and bow. Somebody tosses the Foxtail straight up and the other player catches it (need I say, by the tail only?)

Then the two players alternate as they grab the tail hand-over-hand down towards the ball. The winner is the one who ends up grabbing the ball.

The Basic Idea

Players throw the Foxtail back and forth, trying to catch incoming Foxtails for points while attempting to land their own throws uncaught in their opponent's box. Catches can be made anywhere on the field, but throws must come from inside the boxes. A penalty is taken for bad throws that don't land inside the target box, and a bonus is awarded for good throws that go uncaught.

The game can be played singles (two players) or doubles (four).

The Field

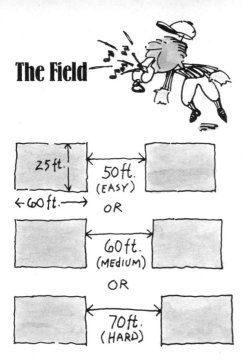

25 ft.

← 60 ft. →

50 ft.
(EASY)

OR

60 ft.
(MEDIUM)

OR

70 ft.
(HARD)

Mark off two boxes as shown. Separate them either by 50 feet (easy), 60 feet (medium), or 70 feet (hard). If it's windy, try to mark the boxes so that neither side has an advantage.

Scoring

Most points are scored by catching the Foxtail, either inside the box or outside, it doesn't matter. How many points depends on how close to the ball the catch is made. The diagram shows how it works. Note that seam catches are worth either 2 or 4 points, depending on which seam is caught.

A penalty point is *taken* from your score if your throw goes uncaught and misses the target box. (and it *is* possible to go negative.)

A single point is *added* to your score if your throw goes uncaught and lands *inside* your opponent's box.

Zero!?

5

4

3

2

1

How to Win

First to 21 is the winner. But note this. You have to score *exactly* 21. If you go over, you have to go back to zero. For example: You have 19 points and you catch by the top color, the one closest to the ball. That gives you 24 points. You're over 21 so back you go to zero.

A match consists of 2 games. Alternate sides to compensate for the wind, sun, etc.

Line Calls

If a throw lands on the line, it is *in* the box. Note that any part of the Foxtail touching the line makes the throw in bounds. When you throw, you can't cross the line, or the invisible pane of glass that extends up from the line.

PARTLY IN AND PARTLY OUT MEANS

IN !

Foul Catches

You have to make clean catches. If the ball of the Foxtail hits the ground *at the same time* as you catch the tail, that's a trap, not a catch. Similarly, if the ball of the Foxtail hits your hand, but you end up hanging onto the tail anyway, that's not a catch, that's a ball-foul. No points for anyone.

Doubles

Foxtail 21 makes a fine doubles game. Alternate the throws, but the catches can be made by anyone. Otherwise the rules are identical.

Batting

No batting or blocking of the ball of the Foxtail is permitted. In other words, you can't deliberately slap or block the Foxtail.

Stay Put 21

Basic Idea

This is a jungle version of 21. It was invented for those times when you're too tired to run around, but still want to keep some vague score. It can be played with just two, or a complete mob. Put in the "One-Bounce" rule, and the younger kids can play right alongside the pro's.

1. Spread everyone out far enough for a decent game of catch.

2. Pass the Foxtail back and forth. Points are scored in the typical way—catching by the colors. But since there are no out-of-bounds lines, you'll need the following rule:

3. Any wild throws that are uncatchable (by consensus) are scored as a point for the catcher. You can mix it up with fastballs, skyballs and off-speed stuff, but basically, you should aim for the strike zone, so there's no real running around (hence the term "Stay Put Twenty-one"). Of course, when there's a mob of players, you can get away with some miserable aim, since someone is usually there anyway.

4. Use the following rule when you've got younger kids who want to get in on the action. Call them "One-Bouncers." They can catch the Foxtail on a single bounce and receive points the same as anyone else, depending on the color grabbed. As an incentive for going for the extra challenge, if a "One-bouncer" manages a mid-air grab, then double points are awarded.

5. First to a million is the winner.

Tennis Tail

Commandeer a tennis court for this version of 21. It's a game for the lob artists, since line drives are prohibited. Play either singles or doubles. An excellent way to put to use an old playground tennis court with a sagging net and cracked concrete.

1. Separate your teams across the net. Use the doubles lines as your out-of-bounds markers, even if you're only playing singles.

2. This is an "air game." Everything has to be lobbed *at least* 15 feet at its peak. You'll soon discover the potency of the well-aimed skyball that nearly goes into sub-orbit.

3. The game starts with the serve, and alternates on every fifth serve. The server has to be behind the baseline and can aim for any point on the receiving side of the net. Receiver can set up anywhere for the catch.

4. Unlike tennis, the Foxtail has to be caught before it bounces. And once it is caught, you cannot move. You have to throw it from the same point at which you caught it, even if you are out-of-bounds. In addition, you cannot re-grip the Foxtail, or change hands to make the throw.

5. Line calls are the same as usual: As it lands, if any part of the Foxtail touches the line, it is *in*. Traps are also illegal (a trap is when you catch the tail at the same moment the ball is hitting the ground). Ball fouls are another no-no (ball fouls occur when the ball hits your hand but you end up hanging onto the tail). Traps or ball fouls result in no points for either side.

6. Scoring:

- Either land a Foxtail uncaught in your opponent's court, or catch one of his throws before it hits the ground (color is irrelevant). Both are worth a single point.

- If your throw or serve goes untouched and lands out-of-bounds, or if it fails to peak at 15 feet, then a penalty point is taken from your score.

- Dropped catches that the receiver touches always count against the receiver (one penalty point). It doesn't matter where they happen.

First to 21 is the winner and you have to win by at least 2 points. During overtimes, the serve alternates every time.

Spud

This is a street game which must date from the Paleolithic era, but as you'll see, there are good reasons for its continued popularity.

1. You'll need a group of at least four. Somebody is named the "Spud." He or she gets the Foxtail.

2. Everybody else has to gather around and put a hand on the Spud.

3. On a count of three, the Spud heaves the Foxtail sky-high, straight up. Everyone else scatters. Before it comes down, the Spud hollers someone's name aloud (let's make it yours).

4. Now you have to make the catch and yell "SPUD!". If you muff it, you still have to run it down and get control of it before you can holler.

THE SPUD

38

5. Everyone stops.

6. You take three giant steps. You stop. You look around. You take aim. You're trying to throw a catchable Foxtail to someone else. If they can catch it, while keeping one foot anchored, they're the new Spud and it starts over.

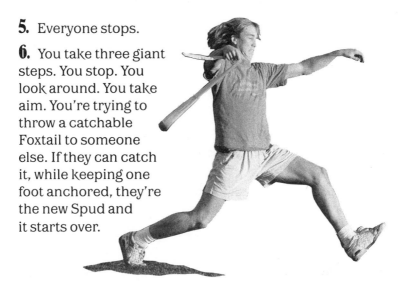

7. But if your throw is way off, impossible to catch, then you get an "S" and you're the Spud for the new round. If your throw was good but your catcher muffs it, then *they* get the "S" and start the new round as Spud.

8. As players get "S" "P" "U" and finally, the deadly "D," they have to step out.

Straight Up Baseball

This is a perfect game for just kidding around with someone. Pretty low energy, friendly but still a game where you want to keep score.

Here's how it goes.

Figure out who goes first. Let's say it's you. Spin the Foxtail hard and throw it as

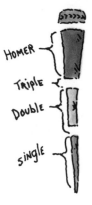

high as you can, straight up. Your partner has to catch it as it comes down. If the catch is made on the top color, right next to the ball, he or she gets a homer. Otherwise here's how it goes:

Top seam...triple
Middle color or bottom
seam...double
Bottom color...single

A miss, of course, is an out. The same with "ball fouls" (when the ball hits your hand coming through, even though you end up hanging onto the tail). And in this game, one out is all you get. Change sides every miss or ball foul.

Score runs by moving the runner along. For example, you catch a double, then a single. Now you have runners on first and third. You get a single, so the bases are loaded. Another single scores a run, and a double scores two more. Then you miss, so you're out, having scored three runs. Now it's your turn to throw, and your partner's to catch.

Variation: If you catch the same color or seam twice in a row, you're out.

Nine innings, of course, per game.

CODY CASSIDY–CF

Double Time Foxtail

This is an advanced 4-person game that is even faster than Twenty-one. Two players are in each box and two Foxtails are whipping back and forth. A situation immediately develops demanding quick reflexes and fast communication amongst team players.

There are two main ways to score points. First, just like Twenty-one, you can land a Foxtail in the other guy's court uncaught. The second method is unique to Double Time. You can also score a point by getting both Foxtails into the hands of the other team at the same time (called "doubling up"). This is the rule that creates the "hot potato" feeling to the game.

Like Twenty-one, Double Time uses two standard boxes, separated by 50, 60 or 70 feet, depending on your skill level.

Set Up and Start. Two teams of two players each get into their boxes. Each team has a Foxtail, which, on a signal, they throw across to the other side. From here on out, until a point is scored, anyone can throw at any time.

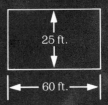

Scoring. Bad throws are scored against the throwing team at a point apiece. However, note the definition of a "bad throw." If the Foxtail lands untouched inside the box, but still rolls all the way out (*all* the way out, so that no part of it is touching the line) then it is still a bad throw. What this rule means in practice is that the roll matters as much as the throw.

Double up's (when one team finds itself holding two Foxtails simultaneously) are scored as two points for the other team.

Drop-in's (when a Foxtail lands and stops rolling inside the target box) are scored as a single point for the throwing team.

Ball catches, the ultimate no-no in Foxtail, are scored as a point against the catching team.

After a Score.

Immediately after a score, play is stopped. Note this though: Even though one Foxtail is caught or down, the point isn't over if another Foxtail is in the air. Only after the flying Foxtail is caught, or it stops rolling, can you tally up to see how the point went. After a score, the Foxtails are distributed one to a team and play is re-started on a count of three with simultaneous throws.

Cancelling points. Occasionally, both teams will score points simultaneously. In that case, cancel the points and restart.

Out of Bounds.

You can catch anywhere you like, but all the throws have to come from entirely inside the box. If you so much as stick a toe out in the throwing motion, the throw is dead and cannot score any points. However, play continues until a point is scored. Sometimes it makes sense to throw from out-of-bounds if you would otherwise be caught in a double-up situation.

The rule on line calls is the same as usual. Any part of the Foxtail touching the line means the Foxtail is in. And

remember the wrinkle about rolling. The throw isn't over until the Foxtail has come to a complete stop. Incidentally, if you touch a thrown Foxtail while you're in your box, and it goes on to roll out of bounds, that doesn't matter. It's considered a "drop-in" and the point goes against you.

Clean Catches. Like all the Foxtail games, "traps" are not considered clean catches. A trap occurs when the ball touches the ground at the same time as you snag the tail.

In the same spirit, if your hand hits the ball, even though you end up grabbing the tail, that's known as a "ball foul" and your catch is disqualified. Ball fouls usually make the best arguments in Foxtail play. The tip-off is usually the sound made when the foul occurs. ("I heard ball!" is the preferred expression when accusing another player of this violation.)

Stalling. If both teams are holding their Foxtails and refusing to throw, the team that won the last point *has* to throw when the other team demands it.

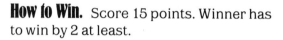

How to Win.
Score 15 points. Winner has to win by 2 at least.

Strategy.
A lot of the strategy revolves around the "double up" rule. If you're holding a Foxtail, and the other team has just released a speeder, loft a sky-high throw back at them. While they're waiting for it to come down, you can catch and (maybe) return their speeder. Of course, the problem with speeders oftentimes is that the other team can step aside and let them fly or roll out of bounds.

If you cannot throw the Foxtail equally well with your left as well as right hand, you would do well to make all your catches with your good throwing hand. There is often not enough time to switch hands.

The key to winning is communication between teammates. While one of you is making
the catch, your partner should be watching
the other Foxtail and telling you
what to do. Either hold it,
sky-ball it, whip it back, or
just loft a medium
lob. The catcher
shouldn't have
to think and
catch at the
same time.

If your
opponents
are crafty, they
will be trying to
throw to the player on your side who is holding the Foxtail—trying to overload him with
a quick throw and catch. As the free-handed
partner, you should always step in to make
the catch, leaving your cohort free to concentrate on the throw.

Foxtail Grope

An easy group game for beginners. Works best with a smallish area and a gang of 6 or more.

The basic idea is very simple. Break up into two teams and draw some imaginary out of bounds lines. (For example: If you're playing on someone's front lawn, the street, the house and the rose bushes are all out of bounds.)

One team starts by heaving the Foxtail in a sky-high lob, hoping to land it on the ground uncaught. The other team races in a mob to make the catch. The object is to catch it while hanging onto one another. (This is touchy-feelie Foxtail.)

A perfect catch is made when everyone on a team is touching one another as one of them makes the grab.

You can keep score or not, depending on your competitive juices.

P.S. Occasionally, a gang of younger kids will only have one Foxtail and as a result end up playing an obnoxious game of keep-away. Foxtail Grope is the antidote. You don't even need to break up into teams. Get the oldest kid (you could even use a grown-up if you had to) then let them do all the sky-high throwing. The object of the game is to make the largest possible group catches. After each catch, do a count-off and try to set the record.

Bat Tail Games

A lot of bat and ball games make the translation into Foxtail very well. The Foxtail's cowhide cover is tough enough to take the abuse, and since all the catches are by the tail only, there's no need for gloves.

When you self-pitch, you can cheat a little on the tail-only rule (just don't get into the habit). Wrap the ball in its tail and toss the whole wad up. After you whack it, it will unfurl and the fielders must make their catches in the usual manner.

You can certainly play regular rules baseball with a Foxtail (just wad it up when you pitch it) but our experience has been that the street versions of the game work a lot better (things like Five Hundred and Over-the-Line, etc.). You don't need as much space to play Bat Tail games, and you don't need gloves. The combination makes it perfect for a scruffy band of less than professional ball-players operating in a vacant lot.

Five Hundred

Perhaps the oldest street game in history. One batter self-pitches and bangs out grounders or fly balls. Everyone else is in the field, trying to get to bat by scoring 500 points. In our neighborhood, here's how the points are done.

Our Neighborhood's Official Five Hundred Points System

500	FLY BALL CAUGHT ON THE TOP SEAM OR TOP COLOR.
250	FLY BALL CAUGHT ON ANY OTHER COLOR OR SEAM.
100	ONE HOP CATCHES (ANY COLOR).
50	CLEAN FIELDING OF A GROUNDER (whether it's still rolling or not, doesn't matter)

All the catches have to be clean. No traps or ball fouls. If you score over 500, that doesn't matter. You still get up.

If more than one person grabs the Foxtail simultaneously, he or she of the higher color takes it. If the ball of the Foxtail bounces off of other people on the way to your hands, that's OK, so long as *you* don't touch the ball.

If any of the players are so young that self-pitching is difficult, you could always set them up with a batting tee (assuming you have one).

Over the Line

If Southern California were a surfer nation, over-the-line would be its national pastime. The Old Mission Beach Athletic Club in San Diego is the holy fount of the sport, and we believe their rules are The Only Rules. We do not presume to change them. The game is historically played on the beach, but any open area works fine. Equipment? One little league bat and one Foxtail.

Around Newport Beach, where the truly serious players gather, fielders are not permitted to use gloves. As a result, the primary offensive weapon is the Warp 9 compound-fracture-causing line drive. By using Foxtails, and insisting that all catches and pitches be made by the tail only, a little of the sting is taken from the sport, but none of the fun.

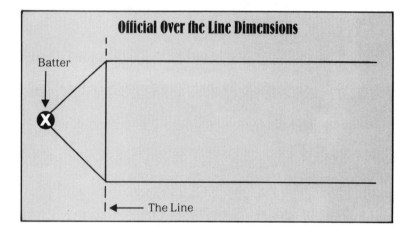

Official Over the Line Dimensions

Batter

X

The Line

PLAYERS.   Three to a team
Positions. Pitcher and batter are on the same team. The batter stands at the X. The pitcher can deliver from anywhere inside the line. The fielders (all three of them) are located anywhere past the line.

HITS.
- Any fly ball that lands fair and is not caught
- Any fly ball touched and not held by the fielders
- An automatic hit is called if a fielder crosses the line while (a) catching a fly (b) attempting to catch a fly or (c) after successfully catching a fly (if carried over by his momentum).

HOME RUN.   Any ball which lands in fair territory and goes past the last fielder, either in the air or on the ground.

OUTS.
- Two foul balls. A foul ball is any ball that lands anywhere but in the fair rectangle. Balls landing on the lines are foul. A ball that lands fair and rolls foul is considered fair.
- One missed swing *or* two pitches that are not swung at.
- Fly ball caught anywhere behind the line or its extensions.
- An automatic out is called if the pitcher goes behind the line after the ball has been hit.

SCORING.
Three hits in an inning scores a run. Each additional hit in an inning scores another run. Home runs "clear the bases." For example: Your team comes up and gets two hits before a home run? The homer scores three runs.

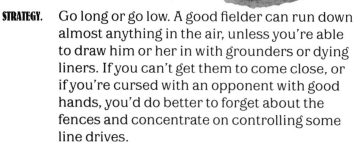

INNINGS.
Three outs to an inning. Five innings to a game.

STRATEGY.
Go long or go low. A good fielder can run down almost anything in the air, unless you're able to draw him or her in with grounders or dying liners. If you can't get them to come close, or if you're cursed with an opponent with good hands, you'd do better to forget about the fences and concentrate on controlling some line drives.

Wall Ball Games

One of the best things about the wall games is that players stay right beside one another. A full-strength game of Foxtail catch is great fun, but it *is* a long-distance proposition. Wall games are a good bit more conversational.

Basic Bounce

You're going to need a big blank wall. We've used a tennis practice wall and the un-windowed side of a school gym very happily.

With two players, back off 25 feet or so and start banging the Foxtail off the wall to get a feel for it. Install a "low-line" below which it is illegal to hit. Figure out how hard you have to sling it in order to get the right distance bounce-back. Catch it on the fly, or on a single hop.

For all you red-blooded competitors out there, what follow are a couple of ways to keep score.

One Hop

1. After you've bounced it around a bit, set up out-of-bounds lines on the court and a low-line on the wall. Use dimensions that make sense for you.

2. The object is similar to handball. Bang the Foxtail off the wall in such a way that the other player cannot make a catch before it hits the floor the second time. (In other words, the Foxtail is caught either mid-air, or on a single hop. Player's choice).

3. You can't run with the Foxtail once you've made a catch. You have to throw it from the catch point.

4.  Scoring is simple. A single point is added to your score for every uncaught throw you can land in-bounds; and a single point is added to your opponent's score for any of your throws that hit the wall below the low-line, or that hit the court out of bounds *before the hop,* As long as the Foxtail hits the wall above the line, and then hits the floor in-bounds, it doesn't matter where it hits on the hop, it's still a good throw.

5. First to 15 is the winner. You have to win by 2. Alternate service after every point and serve from behind the back line.

Wall Juggling

This is actually a cooperative game. You're keeping score, but your opponent is the evil Force of Gravity.

With two Foxtails, and two players, bounce your throws off the wall trying to keep one Foxtail always in motion.

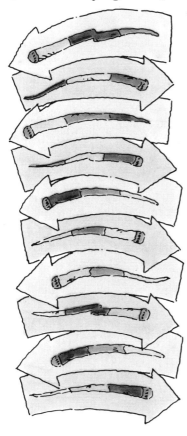

At no time should anyone be holding two Foxtails, and at no time should either of them ever touch the ground. (Hint: Never catch with your non-throwing hand.)

Unless you install the "One-Bounce" rule, this little act is far from easy. But it is possible to get a system going. Our consecutives record is 88, but we're getting better every day.

Foxtail Olympics

This is a collection of events that are designed to test the whole gamut of your Foxtail skills. (Even if you don't have any). Play them to set personal records (PR's), or competitively.

Throw, Run and Catch (T.R.C.). The simplest, and maybe the most enduring challenge. How far can you throw the Foxtail in front of you and still make the catch yourself? All you need is a starting line, a nice high lob, and a winged pair of running shoes. As of this writing, 107 feet is the house record in the unlimited age category. Sixty-two feet for 13 and under.

Field Goals. Recognizing that football fields don't get enough off-season use, we dreamt this one up. On your local high school football field, back off from the uprights as far as you think you can, then take your best shot. With the help of a placeholder, we've kicked field goals of 30 yards, and thrown them 80.

Raw Distance. Just throw it as far as you can For 13 years and under, our current record is 60 yards, in the unlimited age category, it's about 100 yards. No wind allowed and no fair tying up the tail to streamline it.

Accuracy. We've established The Official Foxtail Target to measure all accuracy claims by. It is: One human being, with one foot anchored to the ground, standing exactly 40 yards from the throw point. The thrower then has ten chances to throw strikes. A "strike" is defined as any throw which the human being can touch or catch without lifting his or her anchored foot from the ground. Anything over five strikes out of ten tries has to be taken pretty seriously.

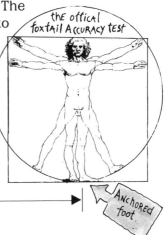

the offical foxtail ACCURACY test

Anchored foot.

40 yards

Obstacle Coursing

Another great game from our point of view since each player will need a Foxtail of their own. Two can play it, although the chaos-factor that a huge group creates does a lot for this game.

Stand at a point together in an open area (field, schoolyard, playground etc. etc.) and set up a four or five "gate" obstacle course.

For example. You're in a schoolyard, standing near the jungle gym. The first gate to your course is simply to get the Foxtail through the jungle gym cleanly. The next is to bounce it off the basketball backstop and through the hoop. Third is to get it over the telephone wires between the 4th and 5th pole counting from where you are. Fourth is to drop it into the newspaper recycling bin and fifth is to get it through the chains on the second swing from the right.

The object, naturally is to run the course, performing all the "mandatories" and be the first to the finish line. Everyone starts at a signal.

Golf

A classic-to-be. Everybody playing gets a Foxtail. Tee up all together and set the first hole by consensus.

A typical game might start like this: You have a foursome. You tee up on Mrs. Pennywhacker's driveway. The first hole is set as Gordy's garage door, three houses down the way. It is, everyone decides, a par 4.

It takes you three throws to bang one off the door. Everybody else does it in six. You're one under, they're all two over. Everyone agrees on the next hole ... through the tire swing behind the Swenson's house, par 8. Lowest score drives first, so off you go. You can play 9 holes, or 18, depending how crowded your schedule is.

N.H.B. Foxtail

A primal game demanding a group sized 4 or over.

1. Someone is designated the thrower. Everyone else is in The Mob.

2. The Mob goes off about 30 yards from the thrower and waits, milling around.

3. The thrower lobs one into the middle of The Mob. Whoever makes the fair grab switches with the thrower. No fair grab? No switch.

P.S. N.H.B. stands for "No Holds Barred."

One Hand Fox Knots

This is a rope trick crossed with a Foxtail. You'll need a limber wrist and a little spare time. People like Mike Callaghan (a one-hand Foxtail knot expert) can do seven or eight out of ten.

1. Start like this, holding it by the tip of its tail.

2. The rest of this is basically impossible to describe, but here goes. Pop the ball of the Foxtail straight up with a little jerk. Now, still hanging onto the tip, hit the tail of the Foxtail with a karate chop just below the ball. That should create a loop which the ball can now fall through.

3. Don't give up. This is definitely do-able. It just takes practice.

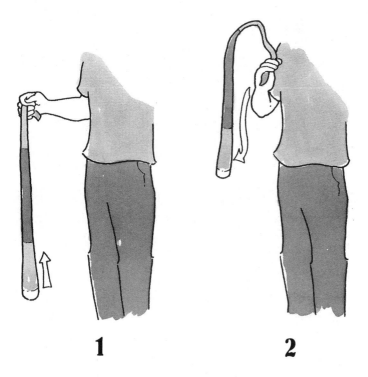

1   **2**

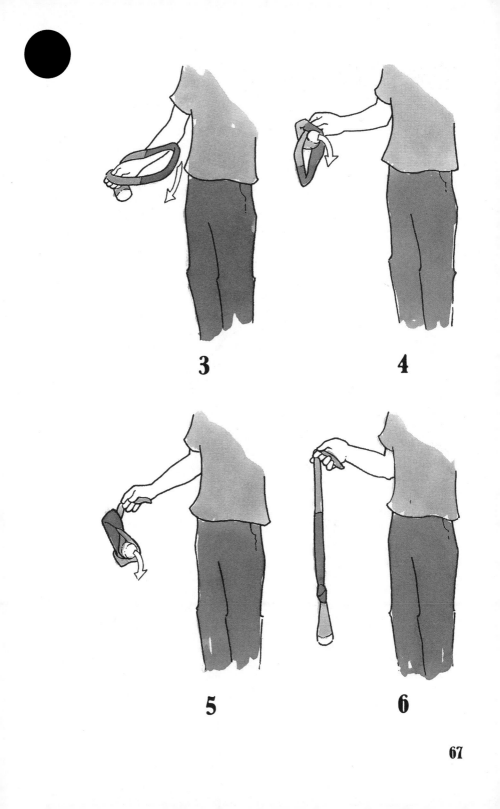

3

4

5

6

Ankle Snagging

This is an outdoor group game with an extremely high giggle factor. Anybody can play. Leave your maturity at the door.

1. Tie a 10 foot length of clothesline to the Foxtail.

2. Gather everyone around in a circle whose radius is shorter by a foot or so than your lengthened Foxtail. Make them all hold hands.

3. Lie down in the middle of your circle and start spinning the lengthened Foxtail around and around, bouncing it along on the ground, trying to snag ankles. The circle should be small enough, and you should be turning fast enough, so that anyone who doesn't jump at just the right time ought to get "bolo'ed" around the ankles.

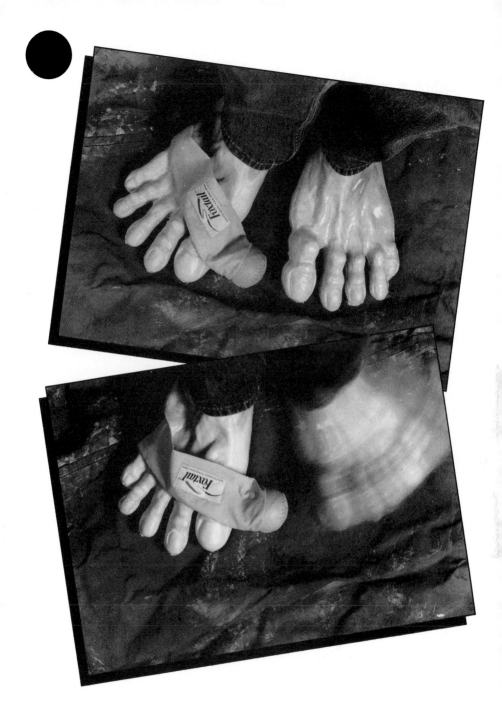

Hot Potato

A timeless classic, tweaked just a bit for Foxtail purposes. Best played with a big group in a picnic mood.

1. Split the group into two teams and separate them by an imaginary line.

2. The idea is to keep the Foxtail moving by throwing it back and forth. As soon as the Foxtail is on your side of the line, the other team can start counting. If they get to 15 (no fair slurring), then the point goes against you.

3. *But.* if you're able to properly throw the Foxtail back across the line—catchably—to someone on the other team, then your team can start counting. Throws have to be lobs, no sky-balls allowed, and players have to spread out with plenty of space between one another.

4. Important point: If the receiver drops the throw, keep counting. He or she can still pick it up and get it back, so long as their time isn't up. Uncatchable throws, however, count against the throwing team.

5. Play to 6,897.

Drop In

A big group game. Drop In is a mix of Ultimate Frisbee and basketball. Our aim is to make Drop In the standard large group game for Foxtail.

1. We play five on a side, but there's no reason you can't use more. Fewer than five, though, starts to make it a little skinny.

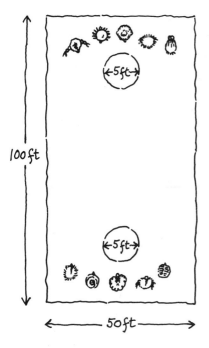

2. We use half a football field, so map out a playing area that resembles something about like that. Use imaginary lines. We're not picky.

3. On both ends of the field, step about five paces in from the end lines, and scratch two circles (goals) about 5 feet in diameter. You can also play with much smaller goals (somebody's jacket, for example) but this changes the strategy a good bit. The object of the game is to drop the Foxtail into the other guy's circle. Basically, the rules from here on resemble those of Ultimate Frisbee.

4. Spread out your teams all over the field (there aren't halves, everyone owns the field equally). Two players in the middle start the game with a "throw-up" (at least that's what we call it). The Foxtail is thrown straight up and both players jump for it. If they choose, they can bat it to another player instead of going for the catch.

5. Once a player is holding the Foxtail (by the tail!) he or she cannot run with it. They have to pass off from the point at which they caught it. They can be guarded by another player or players, but the defender cannot touch the Foxtail while it is being held.

They can also attempt to interfere with the throw by waving their arms around frantically.

6. In order to keep the defender from getting bonked, all throws must be single motion, non-spun underhand throws. Let me repeat that: one motion throws, with no spinning.

7. If someone fails to make a clean catch, or catches it out-of-bounds, the Foxtail goes over at that point. Likewise anything that goes out of bounds. Last team that touches it loses it. If your team is able to bat down a flying Foxtail, it is yours at that point.

8. To score, you can roll the Foxtail into the circle, or throw it. It doesn't matter so long as it doesn't keep rolling out of the circle. If you're using a jacket, anything that hits the jacket counts.

9. Eleven points takes the match, but you have to win by two.

Books from Klutz Press

The Aerobie Book
The Bedtime Book
The Book of Classic Board Games
Braids & Bows
The Unbelievable Bubble Book
The Klutz Book of Card Games: For Sharks and Others
Explorabook
Face Painting
The Foxtail Book
KidsGardening: A Kid's Guide to Messing Around
in the Dirt
Country and Blues Guitar for the Musically Hopeless
Country and Blues Harmonica for the
Musically Hopeless
The Hacky Sack Book
The Klutz Book of Jacks
The Klutz Book of Marbles
Juggling for the Complete Klutz
KidsCooking: A Very Slightly Messy Manual
KidsSongs
KidsSongs 2
KidsSongs Jubilee
KidsSongs Sleepyheads
The Klutz Book of Knots
The Official Icky-Poo Book
The Official Koosh Book
The Klutz Book of Magic
The World's Tackiest Postcards
Revenge of the Son of the World's Tackiest Postcards
The Time Book
The Klutz Yo-Yo Book

The Klutz Flying Apparatus Catalogue

Additional copies of this book, replacement Foxtails, as well as the entire library of Klutz books are all available in our mail order catalogue.

It's available free for the asking.

Name _____

Address _____

City/State _____

Zip _____

Klutz Flying Apparatus Catalogue
2121 Staunton Court
Palo Alto, CA 94306
(415) 424-0739

F

The Klutz Flying Apparatus Catalogue

Additional copies of this book, replacement Foxtails, as well as the entire library of Klutz books are all available in our mail order catalogue.

It's available free for the asking.

Name _____

Address _____

City/State _____

Zip _____

Klutz Flying Apparatus Catalogue
2121 Staunton Court
Palo Alto, CA 94306
(415) 424-0739

F